I WONDER WHY

Leaves Change Color

KINGFISHER

LONDON & NEW YORK

Copyright © Macmillan Publishers International Ltd 2011, 2024
Published in the United States by Kingfisher
120 Broadway, New York, NY 10271
Kingfisher is a division of Macmillan
Children's Books, London

ISBN: 978-0-7534-8049-6 (HB)
ISBN: 978-0-7534-8050-2 (PB)

Distributed in the U.S. and Canada by Macmillan,
120 Broadway, New York, NY 10271

EU representative: Macmillan Publishers Ireland Ltd,
1st Floor, The Liffey Trust Centre,
117-126 Sheriff Street Upper, Dublin 1, D01 YC43.

Library of Congress Cataloging-in-Publication
data has been applied for.

Author: Andrew Charman
Consultant: Michael Chinery

2024 edition
Editor: Seeta Parmar
Designers: Peter Clayman, Amelia Brooks
Illustrator: Gareth Lucas

Kingfisher books are available for special
promotions and premiums. For details contact:
Special Markets Department, Macmillan,
120 Broadway, New York, NY 10271.

For more information, please visit
www.kingfisherbooks.com

Printed in China
9 8 7 6 5 4 3 2 1
1TR/0424/WKT/RV/128MA

CONTENTS

What is a plant?

Plants are **living things**. They come in all shapes and sizes, from tiny waterweeds to towering trees. Plants are different from animals in one very important way—they can make food for themselves from **sunlight**. Animals can't do this. They depend on plants for their food.

Where do plants grow?

There are about 400,000 different kinds of plants on Earth, and they grow just about everywhere—in **fields**, **forests**, **deserts**, and **mountains**. Besides air, the two things plants need are sunlight and water, so you won't find them in places that are completely dark or dry.

Are plants really alive?

Plants are just as alive as you are. They need **air**, **food**, and **water** to grow, and they can make lots of new plants like themselves. This proves that they are alive. Things like stones and rocks don't feed, grow, or have young because they are not alive.

All the food in the world starts with plants. You may eat eggs, meat, and cheese but, without plants, no chicken or cow could produce these foods!

Corals and sea anemones may look like plants, but they are imposters. In fact, they are animals!

Why do trees have leaves?

Like all plants, trees need their leaves to stay alive. Leaves are a tree's food factories. They contain a sticky green stuff called **chlorophyll**. The chlorophyll uses **water**, **sunlight**, and **carbon dioxide** in the air to make a sugary food. The food is then carried to every part of the tree in a sweet and sticky juice called **sap**.

We call plants that lose their leaves in the fall deciduous. Evergreens have tough leaves that can survive the winter. The trees still lose their leaves, but not all at the same time.

Why do some trees lose their leaves in fall?

Big green leaves are useful in spring and summer. They make food while the Sun shines and the days are long. When the days get shorter, there's less time for making food and the tree must live off its food reserves. Rather than feed their leaves too, some trees **shed their leaves** in the fall.

Hungry young caterpillars love to eat leaves because of the sweet plant sap inside.

The way plants make food in their leaves is called photosynthesis. During photosynthesis, plants take in carbon dioxide from the air. And they give out oxygen—the gas we all need to survive.

Why do leaves change color?

It's the chlorophyll in a plant's leaves that makes them look green. But in the fall, the chlorophyll breaks down. Once the green coloring has gone, the leaves' other colors show through—beautiful shades of **red**, **yellow**, and **gold**.

Why do roots grow so long?

Long roots fix a plant firmly in the ground so that it won't fall over on windy days. But roots do another job, too. By spreading out far and wide, they can **suck up** water and nutrients from all the soil around. Then the roots send the water up the stem or trunk and into the leaves.

In the strongest winds, a tree can sometimes be blown right over. Its roots are wrenched out of the ground as the tree falls down with a crash.

At the ends of the roots are tiny hairs, which burrow into the spaces between the clumps of soil.

Why are stems so straight?

A plant needs to hold its leaves up to the **sunshine**, which it uses to make its food. Many plants grow **tall, straight stems**, so that they can beat their neighbors to the sunlight.

Not all plants have straight stems. Some have stems that bend and curl, clambering their way over nearby plants as they climb up to the light.

Sunflowers not only grow up toward the light, but their flowers follow the Sun! As the Sun appears to move across the sky through out the day, the flower heads turn to face it.

A wild fig tree in South Africa grew roots 400 feet (120m) down into the soil. If it were put on the roof of a 40-story office building, its roots would reach down to the ground.

Which plants grow in water?

The giant water lily grows in the lakes and rivers of South America. Its roots lie deep in the mud and its **huge leaves** float on the water's surface. This is the best place for catching the Sun! Each leaf curls up at the rim so that it can push other leaves aside.

The giant water lily's leaves grow on long, strong stems. On the underside of each leaf is a web of supporting veins. This makes the leaves so strong that a small child could sit on one without sinking!

Which are the smallest plants?

Algae are organisms that live in water and make their food by photosynethsis. Although some types of algae grow to be enormous plants, there are other algae so small you can only see them through a microscope. The very smallest float in lakes and oceans, and are called **phytoplankton**. They are so tiny that whales catch millions in every gulp!

The leaves and roots of water plants give food and shelter to many animals. But they are also places where hunters can hide.

Which forests grow in the ocean?

Huge forests of **kelp** grow off the coast of California. Kelp is a kind of **seaweed** that grips on to rocks, and sends long, ribbonlike stems up through the water. Some of the stems can be 660 feet (200m) long—as long as eight swimming pools laid end to end.

HARBOR SEAL

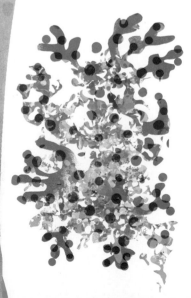

Not all water plants are rooted in the mud. Some seaweeds float in the water, thanks to pockets of air in their leaves—a lot like having their very own life preservers!

Which plant . . . traps a treat?

When an insect lands on a Venus flytrap, it gets a **nasty surprise**! It only has to brush against one tiny hair on an open leaf tip, to make the leaf **snap tightly shut**. There's no escape for the poor insect. The flytrap changes it into a tasty soup, which it slowly soaks up.

The bladderwort is an underwater meat eater. Along its leaves are bubble-shaped bags that suck in tiny creatures as they paddle past.

... fools a fly?

Pitcher plants have unusual vase-shaped leaves that tempt insects with a **sugar-sweet smell**. But the leaves are slippery traps. When a fly lands on them, it loses its footing, **slips inside** the "vase," and drowns in a pool of juice.

Many meat-eating plants grow on wet, boggy ground where the soil is very poor. They need their juicy snacks for extra nourishment.

... snares a snack?

Did you know that flytraps can count? The first time an insect touches a hair on one of the leaf tips, the trap stays open. But if it touches it a second time, the trap snaps shut!

The sundew's leaves are covered in hairs, which **sparkle** with gluelike drops. When an insect lands on a leaf, it gets stuck fast. The more it struggles, the more it **sticks**. At last, the leaf folds over, traps the fly, and starts dissolving it into liquid food that it can drink up.

13

Why do plants have flowers?

Many plants have colorful, perfumed flowers that attract insects and other animals. The visitors feed on drops of **sweet nectar** inside the flower. As they feed, they pick up a **fine yellow dust** called **pollen** that they carry to another flower. When the pollen rubs off on the second flower, that flower can start to make seeds.

Many trees and grasses spread their pollen in the wind. They don't need animal visitors, so they don't grow bright flowers.

This plant is called hot lips—and no wonder! The lipstick-red markings on its leaves are a wonderful way to attract visitors to its tiny flower.

Which flower fools a bee?

A bee orchid's flowers look and smell just like **female bees**. Male bees zoom to the flowers wanting to mate with them—but they **have been tricked**! The plant's just using them as mail carriers to deliver small packages of pollen to other orchids nearby.

During the summer, the air can be so full of pollen that it makes many people sneeze.

Many trees and grasses spread their pollen on the wind. They don't need animal visitors, so they don't grow bright flowers.

Which is the smelliest flower?

The dead-horse arum is well named —it smells like rotten meat! But blowflies love it. These plump flies usually lay their eggs inside the **rotting bodies** of dead animals. They are fooled by the plant's rotten smell, and crawl inside it to **lay their eggs**, picking up pollen on the way.

Why is fruit so sweet and juicy?

Plants make **sweet, juicy fruits** so that animals will eat them. Inside every fruit is one or more seeds. When an animal swallows the fruit, it swallows the seeds as well. These pass through its body, and fall out in its **droppings**. In such good soil, the seeds soon start to grow into **new plants**!

You often see seeds floating through the air. Dandelion seeds grow their own fluffy parachutes. And sycamore seeds have wings that spin them to the ground like tiny helicopters.

Which plant shoots slime?

The Mediterranean squirting cucumber has a special way of spreading its seeds. As the fruit grows, it fills with a **slimy juice**. Day by day, the fruit grows fuller and fuller until it **bursts**, flinging the seeds far out into the air.

The cotton-top tamarin lives in the South American rain forest. It feeds mainly on fruit, especially delicious, juicy figs.

Which seeds sail away?

Coconut palms grow near the sea, so the ripe coconuts often fall into the water. Protected by their **hard shells**, they float out to sea. After several weeks or months, they are washed up onto a beach, where they **sprout and start to grow**.

Fruits come in many different colors, but most animals seem to like red ones the best!

Which fruit gets forgotten?

Many animals feed on acorns, the fruits of the oak tree. Squirrels enjoy them so much that, **every fall**, they bury some in the ground as a snack for when food is short in winter. The trouble is, the animals often forget where they have hidden their supply, so when spring comes the young oaks **start to grow**.

When does a seed begin to grow?

Inside every seed is the **tiny beginning** of a new plant. This starts to grow when the soil around the seed is warm and damp. At first, the baby plant feeds on a **supply of food** inside the seed. But as soon as its first leaves open, it begins to make food for itself.

The seed of the horse-chestnut tree has a tough brown coat. This rots away in the winter, and the young plant bursts through in the spring.

1 The runner bean seed swells with water, and splits open. A root starts to grow.

2 Tiny hairs grow out from the branches of the root.

3 A shoot appears. It grows up toward the light.

Do all plants grow from seeds?

Strawberry plants don't need seeds to produce new plants. They can send out side shoots, called runners. Where these touch the ground, **roots begin to grow**—then leaves and stems. In just a few weeks, there's **a brand new plant**!

The coco-de-mer palm tree grows the largest seeds. They weigh 45 pounds (20kg)—as much as a big bag of potatoes.

Which plant grows the fastest?

The bamboo plant is the **fastest-growing** plant in the world. Some kinds can grow almost 3 feet (1m) a day. At that rate, they would reach the roof of a two-story house in a single week!

4 The shoot grows leaves. Now the new runner bean plant can make food for itself.

Are fungi plants?

Fungi aren't really plants at all. They look like plants, and they grow in the same sort of places. But, unlike plants, they don't have **leaves**, **stems**, or **roots**, and they don't make their food from sunlight. A fungus grows by soaking up food from dead animals and plants.

Scientists have found more than 100,000 different types of fungi—and there are probably thousands more. The tiny, bright blue toadstools shown here grow in New Zealand.

BLUE MUSHROOM

What puffs out of a puffball?

A puffball is a kind of fungus that looks like **a large creamy ball**. If you knock a ripe one, a cloud of dust puffs out of the top. This dust is really millions of tiny specks called **spores**. Spores do the same job as seeds. If they land in rich soil, they will grow into brand-new puffballs.

Fungi don't just grow outdoors, they also live on our bodies! The human foot is home to almost 200 types of fungi. They are harmless, but in some cases cause infections like Athlete's Foot, which creates itchy patches on your skin.

Which fungus looks like a lion?

Lion's mane mushroom has dangling spines that look like a long, white beard or a lion's mane. It is found growing on **beech**, **oak**, and **birch** trees.

LION'S MANE MUSHROOM

One kind of fungus not only feeds on dead animals—it kills them first! The tiny spores grow inside live ants, feeding on the juicy parts of their bodies. Soon, nothing is left but an ant's dry skeleton, with the toadstools growing out of it.

Did you know that the blue strands in some cheeses are a kind of fungus?

Why do stinging nettles sting?

Stinging is another way plants protect themselves. Each leaf on a nettle is covered with small hairs as **sharp as glass**. If an animal sniffs one, the hair pricks the animal's nose and injects a drop of painful poison—**ouch**! It won't stick around to eat that leaf!

Milkweed is a poisonous plant, but the caterpillars of the monarch butterfly eat it and come to no harm. It even makes the caterpillars poisonous —so they don't get eaten by birds.

Which plants look like pebbles?

Pebble plants grow in the desert in southern Africa. They have two thick, **juicy leaves** that any animal would love to eat. But the plant protects itself by blending in with the background. Its leaves are disguised to look so **pebble like** that animals pass it by.

Why do trees have thorns?

The leaves on the lowest branches of a holly tree are the prickliest, to stop animals nibbling them. Higher up, the leaves are out of reach, so they are a lot less spiny.

Trees such as the acacia have thorns to **keep plant-eating animals away**, but they don't always work. Goats, camels, and giraffes, for example, have tough lips and mouths and long, curling tongues to get round the thorns. The plants will have to come up with **another trick**!

Which plants hitch a ride to the light?

In rain forests the tallest trees spread out their branches in the sunshine, **making it shady** down below. Because of this, some smaller plants don't get enough light. A group of plants called **epiphytes** have solved the problem by perching high on the branches of trees and growing up there instead.

EPIPHYTES

Which plant has a private pool?

BROMELIAD

Bromeliads are epiphytes that grow high up on rain forest trees. They don't use roots to collect water—every time it rains, the plants **catch drops of water** in a pool in the middle of their leaves. The tiny pools are perfect for tree frogs to relax in, too!

It's so wet in a rain forest that many plants have leaves with downward-pointing tips. They are like drainpipes for the rain to run down.

Lianas are climbing plants that dangle from rain forest trees. Some animals use them as ropes, and swing on them through the trees.

Which plants strangle and squeeze?

Not all epiphytes collect water in their leaves. Some, such as orchids, have long trailing roots, which soak up water from the steamy air like a sponge.

The strangler fig is well-named because it **strangles other trees** to death! Its seed sprouts high up on the branch of a tree. Week by week, **its roots grow longer**—wrapping around the branches, down the trunk, and into the ground. The fig now sucks all the goodness out of the soil, starving its host until it dies.

Can plants grow in a desert?

Plants can grow in a desert, but they need **special ways to survive**. Cacti have spreading roots that slurp up any rain as soon as it falls. Then they take great care of the water, storing it inside their **juicy stems**. It may have to last them weeks, months, or even years.

A gila woodpecker makes a cool nest for itself by carving out a hole in a cactus. When it leaves, there's a long queue of other birds who would like to move in!

Can you pick fruit in the desert?

Huge bunches of **sweet**, **sticky dates** dangle from palm trees, beside springs in the deserts of Africa and the Middle East. People have been picking the **delicious fruit** in these areas for more than 5,000 years.

Can you find flowers in the desert?

Daisies, poppies, and many other plants flower in the desert. The plants wither and die during the hot, dry months, but their **seeds survive** in the ground. When it rains, they soon spring into action. They grow into new plants and cover the dry desert with a beautiful **carpet of flowers** within a few weeks.

Which are the tastiest plants?

Spices are made from plants. They have such a strong smell and taste that we use them in cooking to give food a kick! After being harvested, most spices can be **dried** and then **crushed** to a powder that you can add to your food.

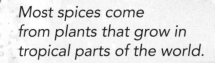

Most spices come from plants that grow in tropical parts of the world.

Why do carrot plants grow carrots?

Carrot plants live for **just two years**. In the first year they make food, which they store in a thick orange root. They use up the food in the second year, while they are growing flowers and seeds—as long as the carrots haven't already been dug up!

Spices are made from different parts of plants. Pepper comes from berries, cinnamon from bark, and ginger from a root.

Do people ever eat grass?

Scientists can improve seeds so that they grow into stronger, healthier plants. This helps farmers to grow bigger and better crops.

Wheat, **rice**, **corn**, **barley**, **oats**, and **rye** are just some of the grasses that people eat all over the world. We don't eat the leaves like cows and other animals do. We harvest the seeds. Then we either eat them whole, or grind them into flour to make pasta, bread, and other important foods.

Why are plants disappearing?

Almost **600 plant species** have gone **extinct** in the past 250 years, and there are hundreds more under threat. People are destroying the places where they grow to build cities and create farmland. **Global warming** is changing the weather, making it harder for plants to survive in nature.

What are plants good for today?

Today's plants are still giving us the **food and oxygen** we need to survive. They also help us to make lots of useful things, such as paper, clothes, and medicines. Every year, scientists discover **new plants**, and new ways to use them. So **let's protect our plants**.

All sorts of useful things are made from rubber. It comes from the sticky juices of the rubber tree.

In some parts of the world, people run their cars on fuels made from corn, potato, and sugarcane plants.

COTTON

FLAX

Linen is made from the stems of the flax plant.

Many of the medicines we buy at the drugstore are made from plants.

Cotton cloth is made from the soft hairs that surround the cotton plant's seeds.

INDEX